Would You Rather?

150 Wild & Wacky Choices

by Conn McQuinn
illustrated by Peter Georgeson

Troll

Have you ever needed to make a hard choice?

Sometimes you have to choose between two really good things, like going to a party or going to a movie. Other times you might have to decide between two things you'd rather *not* do, like taking a pop quiz or doing extra homework. (Either way, you lose!)

This book offers you 150 pairs of alternatives and asks you to choose one or the other. Some choices may be easy for you, but some definitely won't be. Once you've made your decisions, ask your friends the same questions. See if you can guess what their answers will be. You may be surprised!

Would You Rather...

1 Go to Disneyland, **or** get a new cat or dog?

2 Spend a week without TV, **or** be grounded for a week?

3 Have your principal come to dinner at your house, **or** accidentally call your teacher "Mom"?

Would You Rather...

4   Win a big competition at school and get
interviewed on TV, *or* find $1,000?

Would You Rather...

5 Spend the day doing yard work, *or* baby-sitting your little brother or sister?

6 Go to the movies, *or* have your best friend spend the night?

Would You Rather...

7 Discover that your underwear is showing in the class picture, **or** get your hair cut at home and have your mother accidentally shave a spot right on top?

8 Break your arm, **or** your Nintendo?

Would You Rather...

9 Play guitar for a world-famous rock band, **or** win a gold medal at the Olympics?

Would You Rather...

10   Discover that you bit through a worm in an apple, **or** take a big gulp of milk and find out it was really spoiled?

Would You Rather...

11   Move to another state where you don't know anybody, *or* get held back a grade?

12   Go to an all-you-can-eat pizza restaurant, *or* an all-you-can-eat ice cream restaurant?

13 Find out you did the wrong homework assignment, **or** forget to tell your parents about an important phone message?

14 Get invited to a birthday party, **or** spend the afternoon at the zoo?

Would You Rather...

15 Have to stand in front of the whole school at an assembly and sing a song, **or** have a picture of you as a naked baby on the school bulletin board?

16 Be able to play a musical instrument, **or** be good at sports?

Would You Rather...

17 Get good grades, *or* have lots of friends?

18 Get locked overnight in a museum exhibit full of dinosaur skeletons, *or* in a big aquarium?

19 Have your own computer, *or* your own telephone?

20 Spill grape juice on your parents' new carpet, *or* have your parents tell your class cute stories about when you were a baby?

Would You Rather...

21 Spend the day sick in bed on your birthday, *or* on Christmas?

Would You Rather...

22 Go to a baseball game, **or** a science museum?

23 Play a board game, *or* shoot baskets?

24 Be able to read a whole book in five minutes, *or* run sixty miles an hour?

Would You Rather...

25 Have to baby-sit a friend's pet snake, **or** pet tarantula?

26 Have a horse, **or** a motorbike?

27 Be a dog, **or** a cat?

Would You Rather...

28 Be able to fly, *or* talk to animals?

Would You Rather...

29 Have your own cellular phone, **or** your own video camera?

Would You Rather...

30 Go skiing, **or** surfing?

31 Lose your ticket in line at the movies, **or** forget to bring a present to a birthday party?

32 Be able to program computer games, **or** write music?

33 Be a guest star on *Sabrina,* **or** *America's Funniest Home Videos*?

34 Learn to ski, *or* scuba dive?

Would You Rather...

35 Be a lion, *or* a rhinoceros?

36 Be a dolphin, *or* an eagle?

37 Find out that your best friend likes the same boy (or girl) that you do, *or* that your best friend thinks the boy (or girl) you like is a total dork?

Would You Rather...

38 Go to the mall, **or** go swimming at the pool?

39 Get to eat whatever you want for dinner every night, **or** stay up as late as you want to every night?

Would You Rather...

40 Be the best in your class at math, **or** the best in drawing?

41 Have your own butler for a year, **or** your own chauffeur?

42 Have your teacher mistakenly accuse you of cheating, **or** lose a really important homework assignment on the way to school?

43 Be Godzilla, **or** King Kong?

Would You Rather...

44 Get great seats at the Super Bowl, **or** at your favorite band's concert?

45 Have all the pets you want, **or** all the video games you want?

Would You Rather...

46 Slip and land in a puddle at recess, **or** laugh and blow milk out your nose at lunch?

Would You Rather...

47 Climb a mountain, *or* explore a cave?

Would You Rather...

48 Be really liked by your teachers, **or** by the kids in your class?

49 Have five older brothers, **or** five older sisters?

50 Have five younger brothers, **or** five younger sisters?

Would You Rather...

51 Have a home video arcade, **or** a home movie theater?

52 Have your best friend spend the night at your house, **or** spend the night at your best friend's house?

Would You Rather...

53 Be a figure-skating star, **or** a TV star?

54 Have to take accordion lessons, **or** tap-dancing lessons?

Would You Rather...

55 Get a free year's supply of comic books, **or** candy?

56 Skip your birthday, **or** spend an extra week in school?

Would You Rather...

57 Meet the President, **or** your favorite
singing group?

58 Sing the National Anthem at the first game of
the World Series, **or** be a guest on your favorite
television show?

Would You Rather...

59 Hand-scrub the kitchen floor, **or** clean out the cat's litter box?

60 Spend a week traveling in a big motor home,
or stay in a nice hotel for a week?

61 Be Snoopy, *or* Garfield?

62 Be Bugs Bunny, *or* the Tasmanian Devil?

63 Be turned into a rat, *or* a worm?

64 Discover a new dinosaur fossil, *or* a new comet?

65 Split the back of your pants at a party, *or* accidentally burp really loudly during a silent moment at a school assembly?

Would You Rather...

66 Get sent to the principal's office, **or** have a note sent home to your parents?

67 Have your own video camera, **or** your own pinball machine?

Would You Rather...

68 Try to sneak a piece of sticky candy in class and have your teeth get stuck together just before the teacher calls on you, **or** find out the chocolate bars you hid melted all over the inside of your desk?

69 Have your own personal jet, **or** your own yacht?

Would You Rather...

70 Be able to travel into the past, **or** predict the future?

71 Meet George Washington, **or** Abraham Lincoln?

72 Play laser tag, **or** baseball?

13 Go whale watching, *or* jet skiing?

14 Have your own backyard swimming pool, **or** your own basketball court?

Would You Rather...

75 Find out your favorite TV show was canceled, **or** be sick during spring vacation?

76 Pull out your "Show and Tell" in front of the class and discover you brought a bag with your underwear in it, **or** have to go to school with a Barney shirt on?

Would You Rather...

77 See a movie, **or** a play on Broadway?

78 Spill a bottle of really strong perfume on yourself just before leaving for school, **or** find out you wore a pair of pants with a hole in the back all day?

Would You Rather...

79 Accidentally superglue yourself to your seat in class, **or** glue your finger to your nose?

Would You Rather...

80 Play chess, *or* poker?

Would You Rather...

81 Go camping and wake up with a rattlesnake on your sleeping bag, **or** a cougar outside your tent?

82 Win a ten-minute shopping spree in a candy store, **or** get to choose 100 pounds worth of toys?

Would You Rather...

83 Be able to make things move just by thinking about it, **or** walk through walls?

84 Be able to breathe underwater, **or** see like an eagle?

85 Go for a ride in the Goodyear blimp, *or* in a submarine?

Would You Rather...

86 Have your own laser, **or** your own telescope?

Would You Rather...

87 Swing at a piñata at a friend's birthday party and hit his dad in the nose, **or** try to "Pin the Tail on the Donkey" but stick his cute older sister (or brother) in the rear end?

88 Have a radio-controlled airplane, **or** a kayak?

Would You Rather...

89 Eat chocolate pudding with ketchup on top, **or** a hot dog with whipped cream?

90 Have to wear clothes that look really stupid, **or** clothes that smell really bad?

Would You Rather...

91 Go bungee jumping, **or** sky diving?

Would You Rather...

92 Be a werewolf, *or* a vampire?

Would You Rather...

93 Have ghosts in your attic, **or** bats?

94 Throw a water balloon at a friend but hit your cranky neighbor instead, **or** spill an entire extra-large milkshake in your parents' new car?

Would You Rather...

95 Get permission to sleep in your tree house for a week, **or** get to go on a camping trip with your friends?

96 Have pink-and-orange striped teeth, **or** purple-and-green polka-dot hair?

Would You Rather...

97 Be covered with fur, *or* have antennae?

98 Travel to Mars, **or** sail around the world?

Would You Rather...

99   Have a pet rabbit, *or* a pet iguana?

100   Drink milk with salt, *or* soda with salt?

101   Be a frog, *or* a turtle?

102   Eat nothing but brussels sprouts for a month, *or* stay in your room for a month?

103 Trip and get your head stuck in a tuba, **or** your bottom stuck in a wastebasket?

104 Sleepwalk in your pajamas into your front yard and be seen by all your neighbors, **or** have someone tape "I'm a nerd" on your back and wear it all day before you find out?

Would You Rather...

105 Be a gorilla, *or* a cheetah?

106 Walk barefoot across a floor covered with Legos, *or* raw eggs?

107 Be a tightrope walker, *or* a trapeze artist?

Would You Rather...

108 Have a nose like Pinocchio, **or** ears like Dumbo?

109 Work in a zoo, **or** a toy store?

Would You Rather...

110 Be twenty feet tall, **or** one foot tall?

111   Have four arms, *or* four legs?

Would You Rather...

112 Be a ski-jumper, **or** a stunt-plane pilot?

113 Get gum in your hair, **or** jelly in your socks?

114 Walk barefoot over hot coals, *or* through poison ivy?

115 Have eyes in the back of your head, *or* skin that glows in the dark?

Would You Rather...

116 Get a shot, **or** have to take awful-tasting medicine three times a day for a week?

117   Be the star of a hit movie, *or* a hit television show?

Would You Rather...

118 Have mustard on your ice cream, **or** hot sauce on your waffles?

119 Have to eat cold cereal in a bowl of tea, **or** in a bowl of chicken soup?

Would You Rather...

120 Accidentally lock yourself in your locker, **or** get your head stuck under your desk?

121 Sneeze gook out your nose in front of the class, **or** spill spaghetti in your lap at lunch?

Would You Rather...

122 Stick your foot in your shoe and find a mouse, **or** put your hand on your head and find bird droppings?

123   Have ears like a rabbit, *or* a tail like a monkey?

Would You Rather...

124 Eat fried worms, **or** baked ladybugs?

125 Find Darth Vader in your closet, **or** a grizzly bear?

126 Be great at baseball, **or** at video games?

Would You Rather...

127 Spend the night in a freezing igloo, **or** in a creaky tree house in a windstorm?

128 Find your bed full of Gummi worms, **or** corn flakes?

Would You Rather...

129 Cross your eyes and get them stuck, **or** faint in front of the whole school during an assembly?

130 Eat cat food, *or* hay?

Would You Rather...

131 Get a piece of popcorn stuck in your nose, **or** a candy bar stuck in your ear?

132 Eat a live goldfish, **or** liver-flavored Jell-O?

133 Have a green nose, **or** orange ears?

Would You Rather...

134 Find piranhas in your bathtub, **or** army ants
in your underwear?

135 Accidentally spray spit into the principal's
coffee, **or** spin too long on the merry-go-round
and get sick?

Would You Rather...

136 Get fifty pages of homework, **or** eat two scoops of pickle ice cream with ketchup on top?

Would You Rather...

137 Do an awful belly flop off the diving board, **or** do a great dive but lose your swimsuit?

138 Walk into the wrong restroom, **or** have your pants fall down while you're hanging on the monkey bars?

139 Catch your brother or sister videotaping you taking a bubble bath, **or** get caught dancing in your underwear with the blinds open?

Would You Rather...

140 Be Superman, **or** Batman?

141 Be stuck on the bus on a long field trip and feel really carsick, **or** have to go to the bathroom really badly?

142 Ride a camel, **or** a horse?

Would You Rather...

143 Paint a picture so beautiful that it's put in a big art museum, **or** write a story so good that it's printed in a big magazine?

144 Be a window washer on skyscrapers,
or work in a deep mine?

![Would You Rather...]

145 Have your cat throw up in your favorite shoes, *or* on your favorite toy?

146 Be a shark, *or* a whale?

147 Have to read the whole dictionary, *or* the whole encyclopedia?

Would You Rather...

148 Be trapped in an elevator by yourself, **or** with ten people?

149 Be given a buffalo, **or** a giraffe?

150 Have a talking dog, **or** a bicycle that can fly?